People of Destiny

A Humanities Series

There comes a time,
we know not when,
that marks
the destiny of men.

Joseph Addison Alexander

People of Destiny

LEONARD BERNSTEIN

By John P. Reidy and Norman Richards

For their cooperation in reviewing this manuscript, the editors wish to express their appreciation to Mr. Leonard Bernstein and Miss Helen Coates.

CHILDRENS PRESS, CHICAGO

The editors wish to express their appreciation to Mr. Meyer Goldberg, who created the series and inspired the publication of People of Destiny.

Cover and body design: John Hollis

Project editor: Joan Downing

Editorial assistant: Gerri Stoller

Illustrations: John Downs—Hollis Associates

Research editor: Robert Hendrickson

Photographs: From the files of Wide World Photos, Inc., Miss Helen Coates, William Gale Gedney, and Mr. Samuel Bernstein

Typesetting: American Typesetting Co.

Printing: The Regensteiner Corporation

Library of Congress Catalog Card No. 67-20106

2 3 4 5 6 7 8 9 10 11 12 13 14 15 16 17 18 19 20 21 22 23 24 25 R 75 74 73 72 71 70 69

Contents

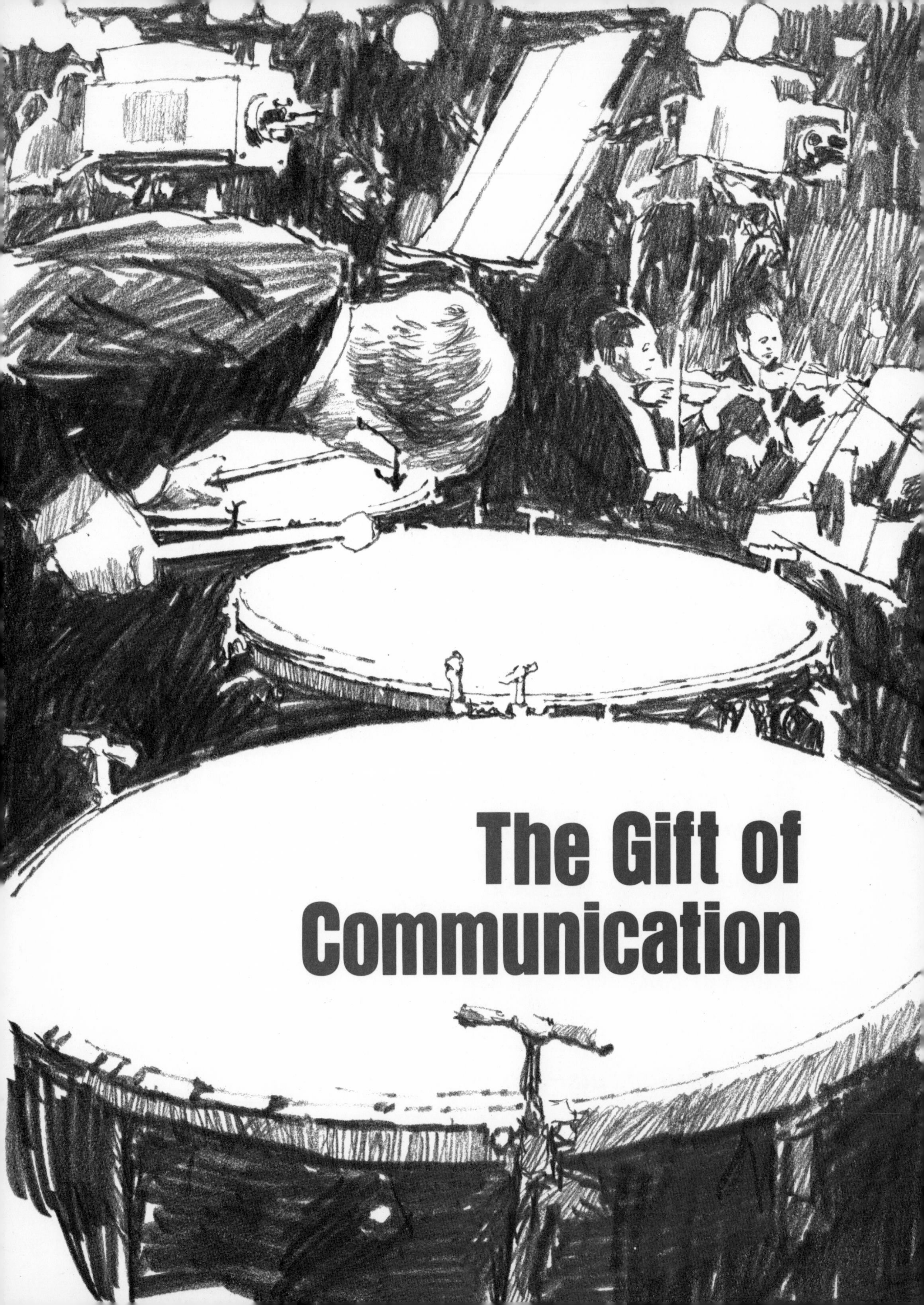

The Gift of Communication

A pale, cold sun shone on New York City one November day in 1954. Doors swung open in the huge building housing the CBS television studios and musicians hurried in with their instruments. The members of the Symphony of the Air, successor to Arturo Toscanini's famed NBC Symphony, were about to perform in a historic telecast.

Television was still in its early years of popularity and critics complained of the low intelligence level of many of the programs. Indeed, much of the viewing consisted of wrestling matches, roller-skating races, boxing, and bad comedy shows. Many television executives believed the American public didn't want to watch anything more intelligent or artistic than this, and few sponsors would back cultural programs.

But the sponsors and producers of a program called *Omnibus* decided to try a daring departure from the usual television fare. They would bring good music to the public and make it interesting by explaining how it was composed, what the composer intended, and how it was executed by an orchestra. It was to be a forty-five-minute special show.

"The public will never sit still for forty-five minutes to watch a music-appreciation program," advertising men scoffed. They had a good point, for many music-appreciation lectures are dull. Spokesmen often oversimplify by telling irrelevant anecdotes that are amusing but fail to convey the aesthetic purpose of the music, or they become too technical to be understood by anyone other than a trained musician.

But the advertising men had not taken into account the lean young conductor who made his way to the podium as the sounds of the orchestra tuning up filled the big studio. His name was Leonard Bernstein, and he had already established himself as the most remarkable American-born figure ever to enter the world of serious music. He was a noted pianist, a successful composer of works ranging from major concert music to scores of Broadway musicals and Hollywood films, and a conductor of international acclaim.

Perhaps even more importantly, he had an engaging freshness and enthusiasm, he was photogenic, and he had a rare ability to communicate with all kinds of people. He could explain music in simple terms without oversimplifying and descending to a child's level.

Cameramen stood poised as the television director counted off the seconds to air time; then the program began. What followed was one of the most stimulating shows ever seen on a national network. Taking the first four notes of Beethoven's famous Fifth Symphony as an example of a theme that was developed, Bernstein then took his audience back to the composer's other theme ideas that have been preserved in his sketchbooks. Beethoven had written down many groups of notes as possible themes before finally developing the famous four notes. Bernstein showed, with the orchestra, what the Fifth Symphony would have sounded like if the other notes had been developed into the final version. By presenting it in this simple, natural way, he made the audience realize the painstaking work that Beethoven had put into the symphony, never settling for less than perfection.

By the time the show was finished, millions of Americans had been caught up in the stimulation of great music. For many it was an entirely new experience, and it opened a new world of interest. The public response was overwhelming, and it surprised Bernstein as well as the television executives.

In 1954 the sponsors and producers of a program called Omnibus *decided to bring good music to the public and make it interesting by explaining how it was composed, what the composer intended, and how it was to be executed by an orchestra. Conductor Leonard Bernstein, the most remarkable American-born figure ever to enter the world of serious music, explained to the television audience the development of Beethoven's Fifth Symphony. He presented it in a simple, natural way so the audience could realize the painstaking work that Beethoven (shown in bust at right) had put into the symphony.*

That first Omnibus *television program, and the many more which followed it, catapulted Leonard Bernstein (shown at left conducting) into that group of celebrities whose names are known in nearly every household in the country.*

"We got letters from plumbers and professors, little children and old men," said Bernstein, marveling at the many kinds of people who responded to the show.

Television and advertising men tried to analyze the reasons for the program's appeal. Some said the handsome Bernstein appealed to women, but this didn't account for the enthusiasm of men. Young people were particularly attracted to Bernstein's manner of presentation, because he was youthful himself, and because he didn't patronize them or act pompous. His natural gift for comedy enabled him to add appealing light touches.

Perhaps even more remarkable was the fact that the program appealed to people at opposite ends of the aesthetic taste spectrum—from the uninitiated public to professional musicians. The musicians were almost unanimous in their praise of Bernstein's thoroughly professional level of presentation. He had succeeded in avoiding oversimplifying, and had acted as if he respected the intelligence of his audience.

The program, and the many more which followed it, catapulted Leonard Bernstein into that group of celebrities whose names are known in nearly every household in the country. The strength of his personality and his powers of persuasion helped to spread knowledge and love of music far beyond the boundaries of the past.

The success of the *Omnibus* programs and the national fame of Leonard Bernstein did not surprise those in the world of music who knew him best. They knew the key to the programs' success lay in the unique gifts of Bernstein himself: his naturalness, his boundless energy and enthusiasm, his thorough professional knowledge, his appearance, and his talent for communicating.

Down through history—particularly in the United States—classical music has usually been enjoyed by a certain group of people, almost to the exclusion of others. The wealthy, the elite, the nobility, have had the time and money to attend the opera, ballet, and symphony concerts. Classical music has traditionally been surrounded by formality and dignity, which has often appeared to be pompousness. This quality has sometimes discouraged ordinary people from becoming interested in great music, and they have needlessly denied themselves the rich beauty of it.

It remained for Leonard Bernstein to change this image for millions of Americans by the example of his own refreshing personality and his solid achievements in music. His *Omnibus* programs marked the advent of a period of tremendous growth in musical interest by the general public. It began to seem that his particular destiny was to share the beauty of music with more people than had ever known it before.

Leonard Bernstein, of course, has gone on to many brilliant achievements and established himself as a giant in the world of music—as a conductor, a composer, and a pianist. He is still a young man, in his forties, and is destined for even more achievements. But however great these may be, many people will never forget that he made music meaningful in their lives in a way that nobody had ever done before.

A Youngster Who Lived For Music

Most musical virtuosos give clear evidence of their extraordinary talent while they are very young. There is a popular story among musicians about a meeting between pianist Artur Rubenstein and violinist Bronislaw Hubermann. "You have talent, my child," said the violinist. "Work hard and you will go far." Hubermann was nine years old, Rubenstein four.

Leonard Bernstein was ten before he had much direct contact with music—an age usually considered too late to indicate the necessary talent for a great career. Both his parents were Russian-born Jewish immigrants and neither had much interest in music. His father, Samuel, was a hard-working, resourceful man whose first job in America had been scaling fish in New York. In the tradition of European newcomers to America, he had striven to improve his station in life and to provide his children with a better education and greater opportunities than he had had.

Soon Samuel Bernstein had his own business in Boston, supplying beauty parlors and barbershops. From a very modest beginning, he built the Samuel J. Bernstein Hair Supplies Company into a prosperous firm.

Samuel married an attractive fellow-Russian, Jennie Resnick, in Boston and they had three children. Leonard, the oldest, was born on August 25, 1918, in Lawrence, Massachusetts, not far from Boston. His sister, Shirley, was born in 1924 and a brother, Burton, in 1931. Samuel Bernstein's business grew and prospered steadily over the years, and the family moved several times in the Boston area, each time to a better house in a better neighborhood.

Leonard was a source of concern to his parents from the first. He was a sickly child, suffering from asthma and forever visiting doctors for one ailment or another. More-robust boys teased and beat him, and he wasn't able to compete successfully in games at school. His feelings of inferiority caused him to retreat into the shelter of his home and for the most part he was a lonely boy who played alone.

Lenny, as he came to be called, had little exposure to music other than the

---

Leonard Bernstein's parents were Russian-born Jewish immigrants. Though his father, Samuel, scaled fish in New York as his first job in America, he soon had his own business in Boston. Samuel married Jennie Resnick and they had three children. Leonard, shown at right at the age of three with his parents, was the oldest.

popular tunes played on the phonograph at home. Probably the first brief indication that he had deep feelings for music came when he was eight. While attending services at the synagogue with his father, he was moved to tears by the beautiful sound of the choir and the organ.

It was not until a couple of years later that he received his first opportunity to express his affinity for music. This crucial juncture in his life occurred when his Aunt Clara moved to a small apartment that did not have enough room for her old upright piano. It was to be moved into the Bernstein house for safekeeping, and Lenny watched it being moved in one day. He hadn't had any training, of course, but he sat down and began to pick out melodies on the keys. He became absolutely fascinated with it. "It was love at first sight," he later recalled.

His parents were somewhat surprised and pleased that he took to the piano so quickly. It was a release from the loneliness and listlessness that had marked his young life. But they began to fret when it became apparent that playing the piano was turning into an obsession with the boy. He would sit for hours exploring the world of sound, experimenting with melodies. He had to be told to go to bed at times; otherwise he would have stayed up all night at the piano.

Since he got so much enjoyment from the piano and seemed to have ability, it was decided that Lenny could take lessons. He studied for two years with his first teacher, an attractive young woman named Friede Karp, who then married and moved away. His next teacher imposed on him an artificial method of hand position for almost two years, and he finally left her because he realized this method was impossible for him. Many years later he remarked that if he had continued with this hand position, his technique might have been permanently ruined.

It was now becoming obvious that he had exceptional talent, and Lenny himself could think of scarcely anything else but becoming a musician. His father thought differently. Piano lessons were all right, but the idea of making a living as a musician was unthinkable to him. He had known poverty and he had risen from it through the business world. He wanted his son to have security and a good income, and the business world was the place to gain these. Everyone knew that only a tiny handful of geniuses made a good living from music; the rest eked out a precarious living, at best.

Samuel argued vehemently with Lenny, trying to make him see that he would probably wind up as a frustrated, impoverished piano teacher. Did Lenny seriously believe he was in the class with Toscanini, Heifetz, or Rachmaninoff? These were the only men who became respected and wealthy through music, he said. Most other musicians wound up in hotel orchestras and nightclub jazz groups. But he might as well have been talking to the wall, for Lenny was adamant.

"I knew with finality I would be a musician," he said years later.

Samuel Bernstein, in despair, cut off his son's allowance so that he could not pay for his lessons. But Lenny promptly

---

When Bernstein was a boy of about ten, he received his first opportunity to express his affinity for music. His Aunt Clara moved to a small apartment and gave her old upright piano to the Bernstein's for safekeeping. Leonard is shown here watching the movers bring in the piano. When the piano had been moved in, he became absolutely fascinated with it. "It was love at first sight," he later recalled.

got a job after school to earn the necessary money, and his father gave in and reinstated the allowance.

Long afterward, when Leonard Bernstein had become famous, his father explained, "I felt Lenny could make a better living from business. Remember there was no Leonard Bernstein then. There might not be another Leonard Bernstein for a thousand years. I'm very proud of Lenny, but the Talmud teaches us, 'Don't expect miracles.' Because God blessed the world with a Leonard Bernstein, it doesn't mean his parents should expect it. You don't *expect* your child to be a Moses, a Maimonides, a Leonard Bernstein. If I had it to do over again, I'd do the same thing."

Lenny, now fourteen, went to play for Heinrich Gebhard, the best piano teacher in Boston. He wanted Gebhard to recommend a teacher, as he could not afford Gebhard's lessons at that time. Gebhard, a man in his fifties, had enjoyed a distinguished career as a concert pianist, and was a discerning professional. After listening to Lenny play, Gebhard realized that he had potential talent. He recommended that the boy begin taking lessons from his assistant, a young lady named Helen Coates. The financial burden would be eased, since Gebhard charged $25 per lesson and Miss Coates would charge only $6. Lenny quickly agreed, even though he would be able to afford only one lesson every two weeks, and soon began to study with her.

This decision proved to be one of the crucial factors in shaping the destiny of Leonard Bernstein. For Helen Coates was the ideal influence in his young life —the person who steered him in the

right direction and prepared him for the opportunities that lay ahead. She was not only a gifted piano teacher, but a warm, sensitive, understanding friend and counselor. She quickly recognized that Leonard was exceptionally gifted, alert, restless, and intelligent, and she encouraged him to explore and seek new knowledge.

As the rapport between teacher and pupil grew, Miss Coates began scheduling Lenny's lessons at the end of the day, with no other lessons following his. In this way she was able to stretch the lessons to two hours or more, to feed his ravenous appetite for knowledge.

He often went to the library to learn to read scores, including those of entire operas. Soon he began to show Miss Coates poems he had written at school and his own attempts at music composition.

"He was frighteningly gifted," recalls Helen Coates. "He could read, sing, and memorize anything. He absorbed in one lesson a piece that took most of my pupils five or six lessons to learn."

The restless youngster was not the perfect pupil, however. Since he could read music on sight, he had little patience for the practicing and polishing of a piece once he had satisfied himself that he could play it. He disliked the drudgery of practicing scales and five-finger exercises. But Miss Coates reminded him that there is no shortcut to complete mastery of the piano, and that the great performers had all gone through this drudgery. She made him develop thorough work habits.

Lenny's parents began to worry less about his obsession with music, because it became apparent that music was changing his whole personality and

helping him to develop in other ways. His satisfaction with his musical ability enabled him to outgrow his feelings of inferiority, and he became more outgoing and confident. At parties he would rush over to the piano and play for hours, which made him a popular center of attention.

He attended Boston Latin School, a venerable institution that ranks with the finest secondary schools in the country. His grades were good—no easy accomplishment in this exacting school. During this time, he organized his own jazz band and took part in other extracurricular activities.

The skinny, sickly, lonely boy had suddenly been transformed into a healthy, outgoing, athletic one. "One day I was a scrawny little thing that everybody could beat up," he recalled later, "and the next time I looked around I was the biggest boy in class. I could run faster, jump higher, dive better than anybody." Now a husky, dark-haired youth, Lenny was a good swimmer, diver, and horseback rider who enjoyed summer outdoor life. But he enjoyed writing, producing, and directing musical shows even more.

His parents had a summer home in Sharon, Massachusetts, near a lake, and it was here that he produced an opera each summer, with all of his friends taking part. One of the productions he and his friends put on was a burlesque of Bizet's opera *Carmen*, with Lenny wearing a wig and cast as Carmen. They also produced Gilbert and Sullivan operettas.

Samuel Bernstein was still not resigned to his son following a career in music, but he began to accept the fact that the boy created interest with his talent. On a vacation cruise through the Panama Canal, Lenny entertained the guests so well with his playing that the ship's captain offered him a permanent job. His father received many compliments on Lenny's ability when he played at gatherings of businessmen and fraternal orders around Boston.

Lenny attended his first live concert at Symphony Hall when the great composer-pianist Sergei Rachmaninoff performed. The youngster was enchanted at the sight of a genius in action. But an even more stirring event in his young life occurred not long afterward, when he listened to a radio broadcast by the Boston Symphony Orchestra. The program included two modern classical pieces, Serge Prokofiev's *Classical Symphony* and Igor Stravinsky's *The Rite of Spring*. It was the first time he had heard any of the daring, inventive music in this vein. These composers had broken away from the traditional sounds of the previous century and devised entirely new music that struck different moods. They changed keys whimsically, parodied older styles, produced dissonant sounds, and did things that Lenny hadn't believed possible.

"Until then," he said later, "I never realized that music had a future. I always thought of it as something that had already been written."

The realization struck him like a bolt of lightning. A whole new world of tremendous possibilities seemed to open for him, and he vowed that he would someday make his own contribution to the future of music.

Leonard attended his first live concert when the great composer-pianist Sergei Rachmaninoff (opposite) performed at Symphony Hall in Boston. The boy was enchanted at the sight of a genius in action. Two more-modern composers, Serge Prokofiev and Igor Stravinsky, had an even greater influence on him, however. They had broken away from the traditional sounds of the previous century, and when Lenny heard their music a whole new world of tremendous possibilities opened for him. He vowed that he would someday make his own contribution to the future of music.

The Hard Road Ahead

Lenny was graduated with honors from Boston Latin School in 1935. It was the 300th anniversary of the great old school, and special ceremonies took place at the graduation. The music for the class song was composed by Lenny, with words written by him and a fellow student, Lawrence Ebb.

It was a difficult year for a young man to go out into the world or to decide his future. America was still in the grip of the Great Depression and millions of men and women could not find jobs. Franklin Delano Roosevelt had been inaugurated as president in 1933, and his administration was trying some bold steps to improve the country's economy and help the unfortunate people who had no means of making a living. Many young men went to work for the government WPA—Works Project Administration. They lived in government camps while they built roads and improved forest areas. Army Chief of Staff, General Douglas MacArthur, pleaded for a larger army to meet the growing threat of Japanese aggression in the Far East, but Congress felt that the country could not afford it. Henry Ford and other industrialists were unable to hire more men in their factories because not enough people could afford to buy their products.

It was a grim time, and the mood of the people was reflected in the novels of young writers such as Ernest Hemingway, who wrote about men struggling against great difficulties, facing failure and death. The lean, spare poetry of Robert Frost seemed to emphasize

The year 1935, when Leonard Bernstein graduated from Boston Latin School, was a difficult year for a young man to go out into the world or to decide his future. America was in the grip of the Great Depression and millions of men and women could not find jobs. Franklin Delano Roosevelt (top left, at microphone) was president and tried to create jobs with government projects such as the WPA. In the middle picture, WPA workers are shown working on street repairs. Henry Ford, shown in the bottom picture at left, and other industrialists, were unable to hire more men in their factories because not enough people could afford to buy their products.

During the depression years, there was not enough money for the government to supply Army Chief of Staff General Douglas MacArthur with a large enough army to meet effectively the growing threat of Japanese aggression in the Far East. In the picture at the top of the opposite page, MacArthur is on the right, next to Philippine President Manuel Quezon, whose country was being threatened by Japanese troops like those shown in action in the picture at the bottom of the opposite page. These were grim years, and the nation had need of the down-to-earth common sense humorist Will Rogers, who had the gift of making people laugh at their own problems. Rogers is shown here (above right) shaking hands with Henry Ford. Ernest Hemingway (below right) was one of the young writers of the day who expressed the mood of the people by writing about men struggling against great difficulties, facing failure and death.

Even though these were hard times, people could still escape their troubles through sports and entertainment, and those purely American pastimes, baseball and jazz, brought pleasure to many. Babe Ruth (second from the right in the picture at left, below) had turned baseball into an exciting sluggers' game with his fantastic home runs. Louis Armstrong (left, above) and other jazz musicians were busy improvising and developing this American contribution to the world of music.

the down-to-earth, no-nonsense approach to life brought on by the depression.

But people could still escape their troubles through sports and entertainment, and those purely American pastimes, baseball and jazz, brought pleasure to many. Babe Ruth had turned baseball into an exciting sluggers' game with his fantastic home runs, and he became a national hero. Louis Armstrong and other jazz musicians were busy improvising and developing this American contribution to the world of music.

Fortunately, Samuel Bernstein's business continued to prosper and he was able to send Lenny to college. He still had hopes that Lenny would eventually join him in the business and take it over some day. In the meantime, a college education was necessary for the future. He and Lenny continued to have heated discussions about the merits of a career in business as opposed to one in music.

Lenny's good grades enabled him to enter Harvard. He majored in music, but took only the minimum number of music courses so that he could broaden his education with courses in philosophy and languages. Unlike some talented people who become narrow specialists in their fields of interest, Lenny's wide-ranging intelligence spurred him on to study in many different areas. This restless intellectual curiosity was to be evident throughout his life.

In addition to his music training at Harvard, Lenny continued intensive piano lessons. After three years of study with Helen Coates, he went on to study with Heinrich Gebhard during his four years at Harvard. He was becoming more and more fascinated with the modern forms of music, including such difficult pieces as Aaron Copland's *Piano Variations* with its dissonant sounds. Under Gebhard he mastered the Ravel *Piano Concerto in G* so thoroughly that to this day he says he could sit down and play it in the middle of the night if awakened from a deep sleep.

In spite of the heavy schedule of college studies and piano lessons, Lenny managed to find time for extracurricular activities. He wrote, directed, and performed in College Day skits, and he accompanied the college glee club. He plunged into an ambitious project for the Harvard Classical Club, composing and conducting a full hour of music for a performance of Aristophanes' *The Birds* in the original Greek.

In addition, he was pianist for the Film Club's classic silent movies, wrote music for the piano, submitted articles to *Modern Music*, a New York magazine, and wrote music criticism for Harvard's literary publication, the *Advocate*, With brashness, self-confidence, and typical honesty he reviewed a concert by the Boston Symphony and its renowned conductor, Serge Koussevitzky:

"By and large it was the typical BSO offering: magnificent precision, the unbreakable tradition of wrong notes in the French horn department, the phenomenon (in the Vivaldi) of seeing woodwinds blown and not hearing them, the remarkable industry of the percussion boys, Our Director's most individualistic concept of tempi—all the things we have come to know and love. One innovation, however; Dr. Koussevitzky has added a tenth bull fiddle, so that the Scherzo of Beethoven's Fifth had something of a Fate in it after all."

Bernstein's first real opportunity to receive recognition by Boston music critics came while he was at Harvard. He obtained permission to stage the first Boston performance of Marc Blitzstein's play with music, *The Cradle Will Rock*. In this production the composer had sat at a piano on stage and conducted the singers when it ran in New York. Bernstein did the same thing in his production at Harvard. The performance was a critical success, and

In January of 1937, the famous conductor of the Minneapolis Symphony Orchestra, Dimitri Mitropoulos (shown opposite, conducting) was in Boston to make an appearance as guest conductor of the Boston Symphony Orchestra. Leonard Bernstein had a chance to meet him at a party (above), and Bernstein was asked to play the piano. This was an important meeting for the young man, for Mitropoulos was impressed with his talent and asked him to attend the orchestra rehearsals that week. Leonard became fascinated with conducting, and it was to intrigue him ever after.

Blitzstein himself praised the Harvard youngster for his conducting, piano playing, and directing.

Blitzstein was not the only noted person in the music world whom Lenny met at Harvard. Through a professor who knew Bernstein, he was introduced to Aaron Copland, the man who was called "the dean of American composers." Copland was impressed with him, and they became friends. Later in his career, Leonard Bernstein was to become known as one of the finest interpreters of Copland's music.

Perhaps the most fateful meeting came with the famous conductor of the Minneapolis Symphony Orchestra, Dimitri Mitropoulos. In January of 1937, Mitropoulos was in Boston to make an appearance as guest conductor of the Boston Symphony Orchestra. Since he would be in the city for a week of rehearsals, various music groups and friends held parties and receptions for him. Leonard had gone to one of these on a Saturday night, but found it crowded and left without meeting Mitropoulos. The next afternoon the Harvard Hellenic Society held a reception for the conductor but Bernstein was studying for exams and didn't plan to attend. As his mother was driving him to the Harvard campus she made a wrong turn and ended up in front of Phillips Brooks House, where the reception was in progress.

"As long as we're here, we might as well look in on it," Lenny remarked.

When he finally met Mitropoulos in the receiving line, he was struck by what he called "the incredible hypnotic quality of this man." They had a chance to chat, and then Bernstein was asked to play the piano. Afterward, the two of them fell into a long, stimulating conversation about music. Mitropoulos was very much impressed with the young man's knowledge, ambition, and energy. Other students told him about Bernstein's local reputation for talent and his many activities.

Mitropoulos invited the young musician to attend his rehearsals with the Boston Symphony Orchestra that week,

Leonard graduated cum laude *from Harvard in June, 1939. One of the Harvard campus buildings is shown in the sketch at left. By now Bernstein had been encouraged by enough prominent musicians to know that he possessed the talent for a career in music, and that he might go far in it. He went to New York, but by the time summer was over he had not found a job and was forced to return to Boston to a job in his father's business.*

and Bernstein was thrilled beyond words. It was his first opportunity to watch a major conductor perform, and he began to understand the delicate, intricate relationship between conductor and orchestra. He also saw how the drudgery of practice paid off. Mitropoulos was able to conduct without a written score. He knew the music so thoroughly that he corrected from memory every wrong note made by the orchestra.

By the end of the week, Bernstein had gained insight into the glamorous job of conducting, but he did not imagine that he himself would ever be a conductor. He still thought in terms of a career as a pianist and composer. But he had become fascinated with conducting through the example of Mitropoulos, and it was to intrigue him ever afterward.

Leonard was graduated *cum laude* from Harvard in June, 1939. By now he had been encouraged by enough prominent musicians to know, deep inside, that he possessed the talent for a career in music, and that he might go far in it. But he faced the immediate problem of earning a living while waiting for recognition in the music world, which might take years.

The old conflict with his father arose again when they discussed his plans. His father offered him $100 a week to start working in the family business. This was a good wage in 1939, but Leonard was adamantly against going into the business and said he would rather starve as a musician first. His father declared that he would be on his own from then on—no more financial support would be forthcoming. It was time, Lenny decided, to go to New York and seek his place in the music world. He decided to try to launch his career that summer. If he failed, he always had the alternative of going back to Boston, admitting he was wrong, and going into his father's business.

It was an eager young musician-to-be who arrived in New York a short time later with enough money to last a few weeks. His first task was to find a place to live. He looked up Adolph Green, a friend he had met one summer in Massachusetts. Green was a bright, witty young man who was to go on to prominence as a collaborator with Betty Comden in writing songs and texts for musical comedies. At this time Green and Miss Comden were part of a nightclub act called "The Revuers," which was featured in a Greenwich Village nightclub. The two young men had become close friends, and Green asked Lenny to move into his apartment with him.

Lenny now had a place to live, and he was quickly drawn into Green's circle of musical friends, many of them prominent in the field. The handsome, dark-haired young man was well liked from the start. His quick wit and his readiness to play and sing at parties made him popular with just about everyone he met. He also had opportunities to visit with Aaron Copland and spend long, enjoyable evenings discussing music.

Despite his popularity and the good times he was having, however, Lenny met nothing but failure in his efforts to find a job. One thing that thwarted him was a rule that musicians had to be residents of New York for at least six months before they were allowed to join the Musicians Union. Thus, it was not possible for him to be employed as a pianist. His money was dwindling rapidly, but though he searched frantically for a job, he couldn't find one. He began to get more and more depressed. It was beginning to look as if his father were right about the difficulties of earning a living in the music profession. He couldn't even obtain a promise of a future job in any part of the music business.

Finally, in September, the day came when he had to face the fact that he had failed to find a way to earn his living as a musician. He had just enough money for a train ticket back to Boston, and he dejectedly packed his meager belongings. It was a long, lonely ride, with the train whistle echoing his melancholy feeling.

"I went home with my tail between my legs," he said.

But failure was not to be Leonard Bernstein's destiny. His hard work and prodigious talent were not to be wasted in the years ahead.

Talent to be a Conductor

Bernstein had hardly arrived in Boston before fate stepped into his life with what was to be a crucial turning point. A former classmate at Harvard told him that Dimitri Mitropoulos was staying at the Biltmore Hotel in New York for a few days. Remembering how well he had hit it off with the famed conductor, who was something of an idol to him, he decided to have a frank talk with Mitropoulos and seek his advice. He hurried back to New York.

The two spent a long evening together as Bernstein told Mitropoulos of his ambitions and his difficulty in starting a career. Mitropoulos told him that he had all the qualities needed to be a conductor, and that he should concentrate on this. But to be a conductor, he would have to go to a top school of music, such as Juilliard. By the time their talk had ended, Leonard was enthusiastic about the prospect of conducting.

The next day he applied for admission to Julliard, but this was September and all the classes were filled until the following year. He consulted Mitropoulos again, and the veteran conductor recommended that he try the Curtis Institute of Music in Philadelphia, which was one of the country's most distinguished schools. There he would be able to study under the great conductor Fritz Reiner, who was a famous teacher of conducting as well. Mitropoulos said he would personally recommend Lenny to the school. In addition, he would be willing to provide the young student with a limited amount of money to help with his living expenses. This solved Leonard's pressing financial problem, although he would have to watch his pennies carefully if he hoped to eat regularly. And he still had to win a scholarship for his tuition.

Ordinarily, September would have been too late to audition for admission to Curtis, but an exception was made for Bernstein because of Mitropoulos' strong recommendation to Reiner. The tense, anxious young man was ushered into a room to audition for Reiner, who was known as a stern, brusque taskmaster.

With barely a pause to say hello, Reiner pointed to a full orchestral score,

---

Almost as soon as Bernstein arrived in Boston, he was told by a friend that Dimitri Mitropoulos was in New York and would be there for a few days. Leonard decided to go to New York and seek Mitropoulos' advice on starting a musical career. He was told by the man that he should go to a good school of music, and shortly thereafter the young man auditioned at the Curtis Institute of Music in Philadelphia. Though it was late to enroll, the great conductor Fritz Reiner (opposite) was pleased with Bernstein's audition and allowed the young man to enter, partly because he had Mitropoulos' personal recommendation.

opened on a music rack so that the title didn't show.

"Tell me the name of this piece and play it," he commanded.

Not many musicians can read a full orchestral score, which may have as many as fifteen staffs, compared to only two for piano music. But Bernstein had always had a remarkable ability to sight read, and it didn't take him long.

"The Academic Festival Overture—Brahms," he said firmly.

"Good," Reiner said. "Finish playing it."

Leonard proceeded to play the whole piece in superb fashion, and Reiner was not only satisfied, but very much impressed. He was accepted immediately and granted a scholarship. After other auditions and examinations, he was also accepted as a student of piano and orchestration. He would study piano under a noted woman teacher, Isabelle Vengerova, and orchestration under composer Randall Thompson.

After the well-rounded intellectual life at Harvard, Bernstein found Curtis to be grim. Most of the students were prodigies who hadn't gone to college and who had few interests outside of perfecting their specialized talents. He missed the "bull sessions" and the camaraderie of college days, and he did not enjoy his two-year stay at Curtis.

But the strict regimen and the rigorous work were disciplines he needed to polish and shape his talent. Reiner poured tough assignments on him with no mercy, as he did with all his students. Most of them feared his sarcastic tongue, which was employed unsparingly when homework assignments were not completed to his satisfaction.

Reiner drilled his students over and over in the mastery of baton technique. He had perfected the use of the baton signal to the point where he could convey what he wanted to an orchestra without having to speak. Reiner's tight, systematic style was entirely different from Bernstein's natural inclinations. Bernstein gets involved emotionally with the music and expresses his feelings exuberantly when conducting. But the basic foundation of knowledge he acquired from Reiner helped him become

During Bernstein's stay at Curtis, he lived in a small, furnished boardinghouse room nearby. His shortage of money and the long hours of study forced him to lead a Spartan existence. He ate most of his meals in a corner drugstore (above); they usually consisted of sandwiches and coffee. The only escape from this routine came on weekends, when he often went to parties given by friends who were musicians and students.

a great conductor, even though it is not readily evident in his style.

Years later, Reiner remembered Lenny as a tremendously gifted young man who needed discipline and training to perfect his talent. He described him as "a human gyroscope." "He was the most talented all-around student I ever had," he declared.

Reiner was not the only strict disciplinarian Lenny studied under at Curtis. His piano teacher, Isabelle Vengerova, knew he needed hard work to perfect his technique, and she was not lenient with him. Anyone as gifted as Bernstein is, finds it easy to gloss over a piece of music without having to put a great deal of effort into making it sound perfect. At this stage, Lenny was still impatient with ironing out all the little wrinkles in a piece. He could play it so well to begin with that he would want to move on to something else. But Mme. Vengerova was stern with him and made him practice over and over. Her demands were so exacting that Lenny dreaded her criticism; years later, however, he credited her with putting the final polish on his ability and making him a professional concert pianist.

"Her greatest single contribution to my development was in forcing me to listen to my own playing," he said later. Many pianists have a thorough knowledge of a piece but play it mechanically, without really listening to themselves.

The discipline in his orchestration lessons was not as severe, and he developed a warm friendship with composer Randall Thompson. Thompson insisted that Lenny had a gift for writing instrumental music, even though at that stage he had not composed much. Time would prove Thompson right.

Bernstein lived in a small, furnished boardinghouse room not far from Curtis. His shortage of money and the long hours of study forced him to lead a Spartan existence. He ate most of his meals in a corner drugstore; they usually consisted of sandwiches and coffee. The only escape from this routine came on weekends, when he was often invited to impromtu parties by friends who were musicians and students. Lenny's high spirits made him as popular at

these gatherings as he had been in New York. He loved to sing and play the piano, often parodying famous compositions or his own writing. Still, Philadelphia was not as appealing to him as his home city was, and he was anxious to return to Massachusetts during his summer vacation period.

The summer of 1940 proved to be a fortunate one for Leonard Bernstein, for he finally met the great Boston Symphony conductor, Serge Koussevitzky —a man who was to be one of the greatest influences in his life. For years one of the country's most important music festivals had been held in the beautiful Berkshire Hills of western Massachusetts, at a place called Tanglewood. Koussevitzky had brought the Boston Symphony Orchestra there for a series of concerts each summer. Now the dynamic, Russian-born conductor fulfilled a lifelong dream by establishing the Berkshire Music Center, a summer school for gifted young musicians. The students would be taught by some of the most famous persons in music, and they could benefit from the stimulating exchange of ideas gained in mingling informally with established composers and musicians. Three hundred young men and women attended the school the first summer, and it soon became a national institution for music lovers.

That first summer, the classes in conducting were closest to Koussevitzky's heart. He had announced that several especially promising students would be granted scholarships to study with him, and Bernstein had applied for one. Strong recommendations by Mitropoulos and other musicians won him the scholarship, and he happily packed his bags and headed for Tanglewood.

It proved to be a wonderful summer. Lectures, discussions, student performances, conversations with great people such as Aaron Copland—and all in beautiful, relaxed surroundings. Students studied while sprawled on the grass in the warm sunshine. They picnicked together, sang, played, and talked about music endlessly.

Even more wonderful for Lenny was the fact that he got along famously with Koussevitzky and established one of the

---

During the summer of 1940, Bernstein met the great Boston Symphony conductor, Serge Koussevitzky, a man who was to be one of the greatest influences in his life. The dynamic, Russian-born conductor established the Berkshire Music Center that year, a summer school for gifted young musicians, at Tanglewood, in the Berkshire Hills of western Massachusetts. Bernstein had applied for a scholarship, and because of strong recommendations by Mitropoulos and other musicians, he received one. It was a wonderful summer for the young man, with lectures, discussions, student performances, conversations with great people such as Aaron Copland—and all in beautiful, relaxed surroundings (opposite).

strongest relationships of his life. The aging conductor, known for his temperamental rages and dominating personality, was a formidable figure for a student musician to approach. He was at the very top of his profession, considered a genius and a unique personality, and he was an autocrat who tolerated no arguments from anybody.

Koussevitzky was impressed with Lenny's talent from the first, and he delighted in the young man's wit and self-confidence. They quickly became close friends, and engaged in long conversations about many subjects besides music. Koussevitzky enjoyed Lenny's wide range of interests and his fresh ideas that challenged tradition.

Koussevitzky was a genius who operated on intuition. He did not have Reiner's analytical mind and methods, nor Mitropoulos' great memory. But he had a perfect ear, and he knew what he wanted in music. His method was to scream in rage at the orchestra until they gave him exactly the sounds he wanted. Over many years of playing together and being conducted by Koussevitzky, the musicians of the Boston Symphony had melded into one of the world's top orchestras, and they understood their erratic, but beloved, conductor.

Leonard Bernstein often tells about Koussevitzky trying to tell his musicians when to start a piece. They sometimes had trouble understanding what his downbeat was.

He said, "Ven my stick touches de air, you play."

Bernstein pointed out, "Now that says nothing, and yet it says everything. When you want an ethereal sound, as at the beginning of the Prelude to *Lohengrin,* a downbeat would be almost too crude. The 'stick touching the air' is really the effect you want."

It has been said that Bernstein was one of the few people in the world who could express a difference of opinion with Koussevitzky and not provoke his anger. The old conductor thought of him almost as a son and called him "Lenyushka." Over the years he was very proud of Bernstein's successes and considered him his protégé.

For his part, Lenny idolized Koussevitzky and set him up as the model he should strive to emulate. His great admiration for the flamboyant genius showed in many of his conducting mannerisms. The big difference, of course, was in temperament. Leonard Bernstein has never been known to scream in rage at an orchestra, or to behave in general like a prima donna.

In September, 1940, Leonard returned to the monastic routine of Curtis and his lessons under Fritz Reiner and other faculty members. He graduated the following spring, and again went to Tanglewood for the summer session, this time known as Koussevitzky's protégé. By the time the summer was over, he had established himself with some of the greatest people in music as a talented figure who would succeed.

But even so, no regular job with an orchestra was waiting for the young graduate. Mitropoulos would have liked Lenny to be his assistant conductor at the Minneapolis Symphony Orchestra, but there was no budget available. Assistant-conductor posts with other orchestras were filled.

Koussevitzky suggested that Bernstein stay in Boston until the next

---

Koussevitzky and Bernstein (opposite) quickly became close friends and engaged in long conversations about many subjects. It has been said that Bernstein was one of the few people in the world who could express a difference of opinion with Koussevitzky and not provoke his anger. The old conductor thought of him almost as a son and called him "Lenyushka."

summer, when he could go to Tanglewood to assist him. He would arrange one high-fee appearance for Bernstein as piano soloist with the Boston Symphony Orchestra, and Lenny could survive until spring by doing musical odd jobs around Boston. The piano appearance would be with the famous Mexican composer-conductor Carlos Chavez, who would guest-conduct in playing his new piano concerto.

But the appearance was not to be. The American Federation of Musicians decreed that union members could not play with the Boston Symphony, still a non-union orchestra. Since Lenny was a loyal union member, he could not break the boycott and had to cancel the appearance.

Bernstein spent a disappointing winter in Boston. His attempts to make a living were doomed to failure. He sent out circulars announcing he had opened a music studio, but nobody came. Two days after the announcements were made, the Japanese bombed the American naval base at Pearl Harbor and the United States was involved in World War II. People were suddenly caught up in these momentous events and weren't interested in piano lessons.

Leonard went to his local recruiting station as a draftee, but he had a long history of asthma and was rejected. Feeling hopelessly out of the mainstream of events, he settled down for a long winter, with little hope for what the future might hold.

Leonard spent the school year of 1940 at Curtis, and the following summer returned to Tanglewood. By the time the summer was over, he still had no regular job with an orchestra. His attempts to make a living that winter in Boston were doomed to failure. Two days after he opened a studio, the Japanese bombed the American base at Pearl Harbor (opposite) and the United States was involved in World War II. People weren't interested in piano lessons. When Leonard tried to register for the draft, he was rejected because of his long history of asthma, so even his efforts in that direction failed.

Valley Forge and Victory

The year or so following his rejection by the military remained a disappointing, frustrating period for Leonard. His father renewed his attempts to get him to enter the family business. Their old arguments resumed. Leonard remained in Boston, giving a few concerts and devoting his considerable spare time to his first professional composition, a sonata for clarinet and piano. In the summer of 1942, he went to Tanglewood as Koussevitzky's assistant.

Finally, in the fall of 1942, he decided that once again he would try his luck in New York, the capital of the music business in America. Armed with glowing letters of recommendation from both Koussevitzky and Reiner, he set out to establish himself. He soon discovered that the letters were of little help.

Bernstein recalled his experience in New York in the winter of 1942 as his "Valley Forge." He lived from hand to mouth, skipping meals when he could not afford them. He gave piano lessons for a dollar an hour to come up with the rent for his eight-dollar-a-week furnished room. But his small earnings just did not stretch far enough. At one point he was forced to wire his father for twenty-five dollars to pay three weeks back rent so his landlord would not put him out in the street.

Finally, in the fall of 1942, Bernstein decided once again to try his luck in New York. Armed with letters of recommendation from both Koussevitzky and Reiner, he set out to establish himself. He soon discovered that the letters were of little help. Bernstein recalled his experience in New York that winter as his "Valley Forge." He lived from hand to mouth, skipping meals when he could not afford them.

Finally an opportunity came. It didn't seem like much of a break but might mean work and a little money. A friend told Leonard about a job arranging songs for the piano at twenty-five dollars a week for Harms-Remick, a branch of the Music Publishers Holding Corporation.

Lenny went over to Harms and got the job. Among other duties, he was required to listen to jazz improvisations and write them down on paper. Since Bernstein had a keen musical ear and superb musical craftsmanship, he could do the job rapidly. The fact that he could do this enabled Harms to get the sheet music out for sale quickly. While it was valuable experience and exposed him to many interesting musical ideas in jazz, Lenny regarded it as hack work. Some of his arrangements were published under the pen name "Lenny Amber."

These daytime efforts of Lenny Amber gave Leonard Bernstein a sense of security and made it possible for him to move into a modest but comfortable studio apartment on West 52nd Street. After hours, he began making concert appearances. He played Copland's *Piano Sonata* at Town Hall; made special appearances at the Museum of Modern Art and the New York Public Library; was pianist on radio station WNYC, where he played his own clarinet sonata with clarinetist David Oppenheim.

Ever restless and energetic, Leonard began composing whenever he could find the spare time. He completed a song cycle called *I Hate Music: Five*

Kids Songs and had it published. The New England Conservatory of Music was sponsoring a contest for a symphony by American composers, and Leonard suddenly decided to enter. A symphony should have a theme or basic inspiration, and Bernstein decided to base his on the Biblical prophet, Jeremiah. Earlier he had sketched a composition, called *Lamentation,* which was based on the Book of Lamentations in the Bible. Now he decided that it would serve very well as the third movement of the symphony. The problem was that the deadline wasn't very far away —midnight, December 31, 1942. He worked feverishly, night after night, keeping himself awake with coffee, and managed to complete the orchestration in ten days. His sister Shirley and other friends helped ink in the notes and write the time signatures on the score on the last day. Lenny himself delivered the manuscript about an hour before the deadline.

It was an exhilarating if exhausting effort—the kind of challenge that he always liked. Unfortunately, the *Jeremiah Symphony* did not win the prize. On top of this disappointment, he was told bluntly by his idol, Koussevitzky, that he did not like the symphony. It was a discouraging blow, and Lenny became despondent. Furthermore, he wanted to make some progress and seemed to be at a standstill despite his frenetic activity in New York. Summer came and there was no Berkshire Festival to attend. It had been called off because of the war. However, there were some Red Cross benefit concerts at Tanglewood by Koussevitzky, and Leonard was invited to play there. Leonard traveled to Tanglewood by way of Boston, where once again he was called by the army. But the answer was the same: he was rejected because of his asthma. He arrived at Tanglewood in a very depressed mood. The following day, August 25, 1943, was Leonard's twenty-fifth birthday, but he didn't feel much like celebrating. He was seriously wondering whether he would ever break his way into the New York music world and have a full-time career.

But that day he suddenly received word from Koussevitzky that Artur Rodzinski, newly appointed music director of the New York Philharmonic, wanted to see him that day at his farm in nearby Stockbridge. Bernstein went over to visit the well-known conductor and they sat in a field and talked. Rodzinski had seen Bernstein conduct a student orchestra at Tanglewood and had heard about him through Reiner and Koussevitzky. Suddenly he asked the startled young man how he would like to be assistant conductor of the New York Philharmonic.

It was like a bolt out of the blue. At last he was going to have an opportunity to be a professional musician—with one of the world's great orchestras. His doubts and frustrations evaporated into thin air, and he knew he had a future in music without resorting to hack work to make a living. In fact, he was offered a salary of $125 a week, more than his father had offered him in the business world.

Leonard Bernstein became the youngest man ever to receive the assistant-conductor's appointment with the New York Philharmonic. A few days later, his picture and a short item about his appointment appeared in the New York *Times*. He tore it out of the paper and mailed it to Helen Coates in Boston with this inscription: "Here we go! Love, Lenny."

An assistant conductor attends all rehearsals and sometimes takes over during them. He also has an opportunity to read new scores, a good way to become familiar with contemporary music. Leonard rejoiced in all these facets of his new job but, of course, he kept hoping for the rare opportunity of actually conducting in a performance. Most assistant conductors, however, spend years without ever getting this chance. In fact, assistant conductors' jobs are sometimes dead-end streets and if the young men in them are to advance, they must leave their posts and go to other orchestras. Even then, vacancies for conductors' jobs are few and far between.

But good fortune came to Bernstein when he had been on the job only a few weeks. That date with destiny was Sunday afternoon, November 14, 1943. A great conductor, Bruno Walter, was scheduled as guest conductor of the New York Philharmonic, but suddenly came down with flu the day before. Rodzinski was out of town, on his farm in Stockbridge, and could not be reached. It quickly became apparent that the young assistant conductor from Boston would have to take over if there was to be a concert—and it was scheduled to be a live radio-network broadcast.

Leonard had stayed up until four Sunday morning at a party given by Jennie Tourel after her Town Hall recital, which had included the *Five Kid Songs*, by Bernstein. And he was deep in slumber when he was aroused at eight o'clock in the morning by a telephone call from Bruno Zirato, associate manager of the Philharmonic. When told he would definitely have to conduct that afternoon, Leonard could only gasp, "Oh, my God!"

In August, 1943, Leonard Bernstein became the youngest man ever to receive the assistant conductor's appointment with the New York Philharmonic. A few weeks later, guest conductor Bruno Walter (opposite) came down with flu and could not conduct. Artur Rodzinski, the orchestra's director, could not be reached, and Leonard knew he would have to take over if there was to be a concert.

"One quality shared by most people destined for greatness is a thorough preparedness when opportunity strikes."

He took the scores for the performance and dashed over to Bruno Walter's apartment where he and the shivering conductor reviewed the program: Schumann's *Manfred Overture;* Richard Strauss's *Don Quixote;* a world premiere of Miklos Rozsa's *Theme, Variations and Finale* and Wagner's *Prelude to Die Meistersinger*.

Bernstein hadn't even had time to stop for breakfast, but there was little time now. He hurried home to study the scores and called his parents, who were visiting in New York.

He asked his father, "Do you remember my telling you Friday that you would have to wait ten years to see me conduct the Philharmonic? Well, I made a slight miscalculation. You're going to see me this afternoon."

As his astonished parents made plans to attend the concert, Leonard went back to studying the scores. Few people would expect a last-minute substitute conductor to give a perfect performance, but he was determined to give it everything he had.

It was time to get dressed and leave for the concert hall. Leonard realized for the first time that he didn't have the usual attire for an afternoon concert—striped pants and a formal coat. He grabbed the next best thing from the closet: a dark grey flannel suit.

His nerves were standing on end as he dashed onto the street, so he ducked into a drugstore for a quick cup of coffee. He could hardly hold the cup to gulp the coffee. The next thing he knew, he was standing in the wings, ready to make his entrance.

The audience hushed as Bruno Zirato announced that the guest conductor was ill. Then he declared, "you are going to witness the debut of a full-fledged conductor born, educated, and trained in this country."

There was only brief, polite applause as the curious audience watched the lean, athletic young man stride briskly to the podium. He looked entirely too young to be a conductor of a world-famous orchestra. He didn't even carry a baton.

He raised his hands and the concert, Leonard Bernstein's trial by fire, began. The first notes rang out brilliantly, and from then until the dramatic closing passages of Wagner two hours later, the audience watched and heard an amazing performance. The handsome young conductor radiated confidence as he led the orchestra through an unusually brilliant and expressive performance. At the end, as he took his bows, the applause grew and grew until it reached a level rarely heard. Musical history had been made.

The radio audience had been thrilled, too, and one of the first listeners to wire congratulations was none other than Koussevitzky. His telegram read simply: "Listening. Now. Wonderful."

When time for the concert came—a live radio-network broadcast—Leonard's nerves were standing on end. He raised his hands and the concert, Leonard Bernstein's trial by fire, began. The first notes rang out brilliantly, and from then until the dramatic closing passages two hours later, the audience watched and heard an amazing performance. Overnight, Leonard Bernstein, only twenty-five years old, became famous.

The newspapers recognized the appeal of the dramatic story of a young man who had made good. It was like a rookie pinch hitter in baseball hitting a home run to win the World Series. The New York *Times* carried the story on its front page and added an editorial inside. The *Times* music critic, Olin Downes, wrote that Bernstein "shows that he is one of the very few conductors of the rising generation who are indubitably to be reckoned with. . . . It was clear at once that . . . he was conducting the orchestra in his own right and not the orchestra conducting him; that he had every one of the scores both in his hands and his head. . . ."

Overnight, Leonard Bernstein had become famous, and some newspapers referred to him as an "instant success" and wrote of his "lucky break." The reporters apparently knew little of the long years of hard work and study that prepared him for such a golden opportunity.

One quality shared by most people destined for greatness is a thorough preparedness when opportunity strikes. Nearly everyone is presented with at least a few opportunities during his lifetime, but not everyone is prepared to take advantage of them. Bernstein was a perfect example of a man who was ready that Sunday afternoon. Never was an aspiring musician more qualified to rise to a challenge.

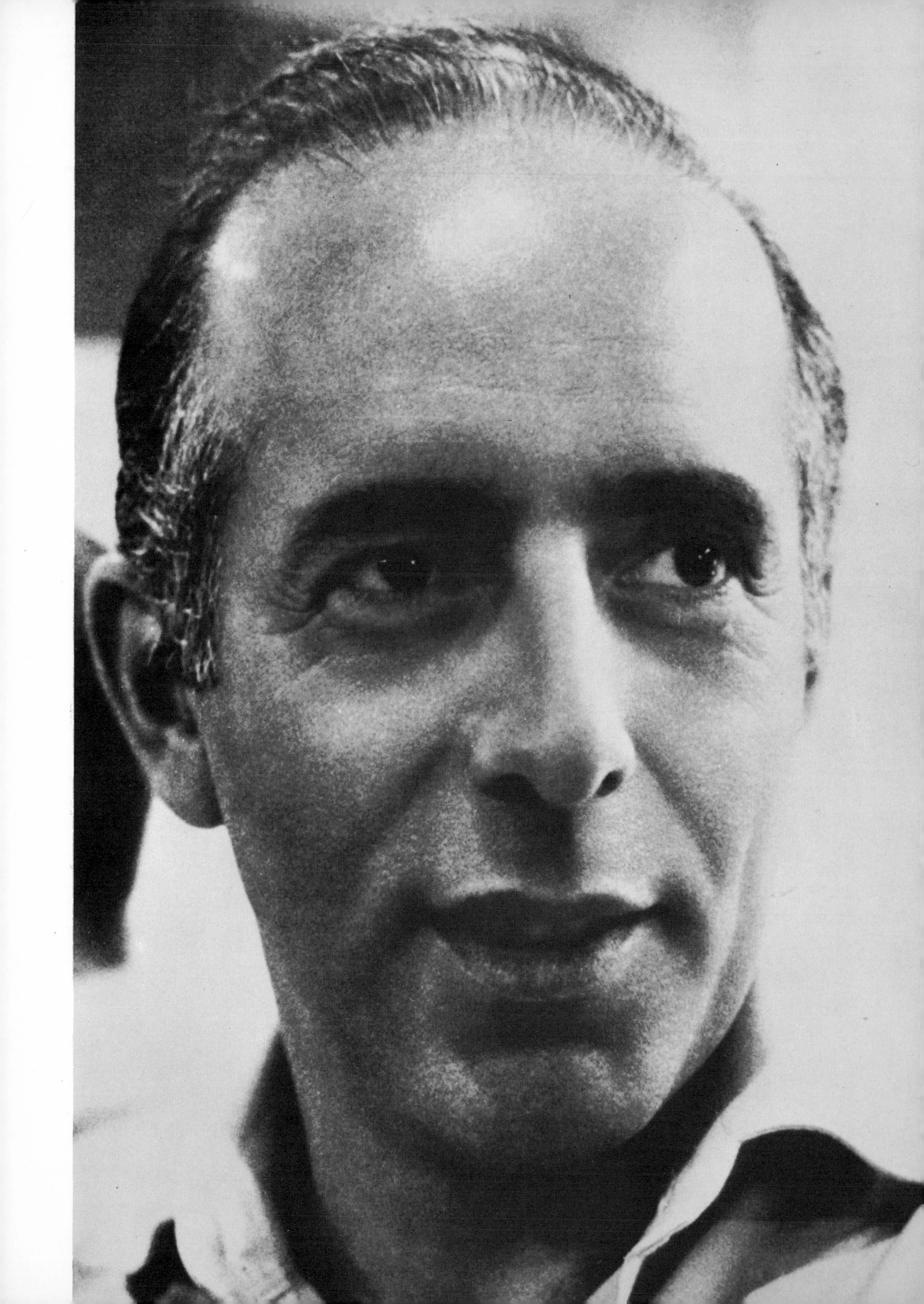

A Celebrity Who Tries Everything

Bernstein had an opportunity two weeks later to prove that his celebrated performance was no "flash in the pan." This time he substituted for guest conductor Howard Barlow at the last minute and once again received glowing critical praise.

Suddenly he was in great demand as a guest conductor throughout the country. In January, 1944—two months after his radio performance—he conducted the premiere of his own *Jeremiah Symphony* in Pittsburgh at the invitation of Fritz Reiner. Later, Koussevitzky invited him to present it in Boston, and during the year he presented the symphony in a number of other cities. It now became apparent that the young Bostonian had advanced too far to be relegated to the role of assistant conductor any longer. In February, 1944, the New York Philharmonic announced that Leonard Bernstein's contract as assistant conductor was not being renewed. Instead, in future appearances with the orchestra he would be a full-fledged guest conductor.

At the end of the 1944 season, Bernstein received the New York Music Critics Circle Award for his *Jeremiah Symphony* as the "most outstanding orchestral work by an American composer introduced during the 1943-44 season." It was the first of many awards that were to come his way.

But Leonard's conducting represented his public side. Away from the constant glare of publicity, he was every bit as active composing. He completed the musical score for the ballet *Fancy Free* under extremely trying circumstances. He and Jerome Robbins, a talented young ballet dancer, were commissioned to write the ballet for Ballet Theatre. Robbins, who was to do the choreography, was on tour with the Ballet Theatre Company during most of the season, so most of their collaboration was done by telephone and telegrams.

Fancy Free was presented for the Ballet Theater's spring season at the Metropolitan Opera House in New York on April 18, 1944, with Leonard Bernstein conducting. It was a fresh, breezy, colorful ballet with sprightly, jazz-oriented music. The New York *Herald Tribune* pronounced it a perfect American character ballet. So popular was it that the Ballet Theatre's season was extended two weeks and *Fancy Free* was performed twelve additional times. In its first year it was performed 161 times.

By 1944, it was apparent that Bernstein had advanced too far to be relegated to the role of assistant conductor any longer. Instead, the New York Philharmonic made him a full-fledged guest conductor for future performances. During that year, he and choreographer Jerome Robbins (opposite) were commissioned to write the ballet Fancy Free, *which was presented in 1944.*

Jerome Robbins' own words probably best describe *Fancy Free:*

"With the sound of a juke box, the curtain rises on a street corner with a lamppost, a side-street bar, and New York skyscrapers pricked out with a crazy pattern of lights, making a dizzying background. Three sailors explode on the stage; they are on shore leave in the city and on the prowl for girls. The tale of how they meet first one, then a second girl, and how they fight over them, lose them, and in the end take off after still a third, is the story of the ballet."

Since *Fancy Free* was such a success, Bernstein and Robbins decided to write a Broadway musical. They collaborated with Bernstein's old friends, Adolph Green and Betty Comden, and went to work on it immediately. As it happened, Bernstein and Green both needed minor surgical operations, so they arranged them for the same time, at the same hospital, and shared a room. It was a lively convalescence, with the two of them arguing, discussing the songs from their forthcoming musical, and singing them loudly. But they made good progress, and as soon as they were released, worked at it so steadily that the show was ready to open a few months later.

It was titled *On the Town,* and the word got around that it was sure to be a hit even before it opened. The film rights were sold to Hollywood for a large sum before it went into rehearsal. It was, indeed, a hit musical, for it ran for 463 performances on Broadway. Bernstein's score was far more sophisticated than most Broadway music, and his tremendously advanced musical knowledge was put to good use in dramatizing the entire show.

New York *Times* critic Olin Downes called *On the Town* "a brilliant, swift-paced affair which brings a new style, technique, and tempo to a conglomerate and extremely diverting satire on New York City."

A short time later, Bernstein introduced his *Seven Anniversaries* for solo piano at a benefit concert at the Boston Opera House. The *Anniversaries* were tributes to seven individuals very close to Bernstein: Aaron Copland; his sister, Shirley Bernstein; Serge and Natalie Koussevitzky; Paul Bowles; William Schuman; and Albert Eisner, his former Harvard roommate.

In May, 1945, Bernstein presented at the Park Avenue Synagogue a four-part mixed voices, cantor, and organ liturgical work called *Haskivenu.* At the age of twenty-eight, the young composer-conductor was earning well over $100,000 annually—just three years after he had been an unemployed musician. He had achieved a material and artistic success his father would not have thought possible.

Bernstein presented a glamorous figure for the musical world, and was described as a musical matinee idol because of his popularity. He possessed a rugged masculine handsomeness, and made a striking—even electrifying—appearance. His continued output of creative effort, however, made it apparent that beneath the surface charm, the engaging personality, and the dazzling gifts as a conductor, there was a serious, well-disciplined, enormously energetic, and prolific composer.

Fancy Free *was a great success, and Bernstein and Robbins decided to write a Broadway musical. They collaborated with Bernstein's old friends, Adolph Green and Betty Comden (opposite), and wrote* On The Town, *a hit musical that ran for 463 performances on Broadway.*

As in his school days, Leonard was much more than a man whose entire life was wrapped up in the field of music. He spoke French, Spanish, Italian, and German well and had thoroughly studied Hebrew and Latin. He loved to read, in a range from the classics to popular fiction, from philosophy to biography. He continued to enjoy poetry, as he had during his childhood, reading it as well as writing it. He continued a concern for politics and social questions, maintaining the same idealistic, progressive-liberal ideas he had formed at Harvard.

In his own field, music, he seemed like a young Renaissance man, attempting successfully to be knowledgeable and creative in several different areas, rather than specializing in only one. His restless energy and ambition spurred him on to achievements in composing, conducting, and playing—both serious music and in the Broadway theater. His old friend and mentor, Koussevitzky, lectured him severely about "spreading himself too thin" by trying to do too many things at once. Koussevitzky was especially upset at the fact that "Lenyushka" had wasted six months writing the musical *On the Town* when he should have been conducting or composing concert music.

Perhaps this censure influenced Leonard to accept a new musical challenge as director of the New York City Symphony. This was a young orchestra that had been beset by financial troubles from its beginning. Affiliated with New York City Center, it was supposed to represent the city, but actually did not receive direct support from the city government. There was no money to pay the director or the soloists, and it was a wonder that it was able to keep going.

Characteristically, Bernstein plunged into his task with enthusiasm and injected new life into the orchestra. He revived long-neglected masterworks and at the same time introduced new American composers and contemporary works by acknowledged modern masters.

Within two years, the New York City Symphony became one of the most exciting orchestras in the country and critics were delighted with its fresh approach to music. But although attendance rose, the financial problems continued.

In the meantime, Leonard continued to compose. His second ballet, *Facsimile*, was presented at the Broadway Theater in October, 1946. This one, too, was done in collaboration with Jerome Robbins. Unlike *Fancy Free*, however, the new ballet did not have a lively, joyful theme—in fact, it was quite the opposite. Bernstein's music had to express a mood of boredom and unhappiness, and this feeling was not natural to the composer of the sprightly music of *Fancy Free*. Nevertheless, the energetic young man managed to create the required feeling in some interesting music.

His popularity had spread abroad, and that year—1946—he made the first of many European appearances. Bernstein, along with Sir Thomas Beecham and Charles Munch, was invited to conduct at the Fiftieth Anniversary Festival of the Czech Philharmonic in Prague. Bernstein's contemporary American programs stole the show from the two more-celebrated European maestros.

Returning home, he gave the American premiere of Benjamin Britten's new

---

Bernstein became director of the New York City Symphony in 1945. It was a young orchestra that had been beset by financial troubles since its beginning, but Bernstein soon injected new life into the orchestra. In the meantime, Bernstein continued to compose. His second ballet, Facsimile, *was presented in 1946. His popularity had spread abroad, and in 1946 he made the first of many European appearances, a conducting performance at the Fiftieth Anniversary Festival of the Czech Philharmonic in Prague. The sketch on the opposite page shows the Karlsbrucke Bridge in that historic city.*

opera, *Peter Grimes,* at Tanglewood and continued to be guest conductor for America's finest orchestras.

The next year he was off again to Europe for appearances in Germany, Austria, France, Belgium, the Netherlands, and England. His trip also took him to Israel, where his performance as conductor of the *Jeremiah Symphony* during the tenth anniversary of the Palestine Philharmonic was well received. That year he wrote *La Bonne Cuisine*, a delightfully amusing song cycle inspired by a French cookbook.

By now a world figure, Bernstein went back to Europe for the third straight year and gave his first command performance, before royalty, in the Netherlands. But even more important was his return visit to Israel.

The Second World War had ended three years before, but fighting and killing went on in Israel. The Jews, who had been scattered over the world for centuries and had been the victims of the Nazi regime in Germany, had at last been given the right to return to their ancient homeland. The new state of Israel was established and the British troops who had been occupying the country pulled out. This left thousands of Arabs who were bitter toward the Jews

for regaining control of a land the Arabs had been living in. Many Arab refugees settled just over the border in neighboring Arab countries and stirred up violence. Soon military forces from these Arab countries were fighting a full-scale war against the Israelis.

The new nation was in the midst of fighting for its very life when Bernstein came in September of 1948 to conduct the Palestine Symphony, which had been renamed the Israel Philharmonic Orchestra. He toured the country with the orchestra, often performing dangerously close to the firing lines.

At one point, he decided to play a concert for the combat troops right in the fighting zone. Thirty volunteer musicians put their instruments into an armored bus and accompanied him to

In 1947, Bernstein again went to Europe, including a trip to Israel where he conducted his own Jeremiah Symphony. *He went back in 1948, when military forces from neighboring Arab countries were fighting a full-scale war against the Israelis (below).*

the combat zone. The enemy spotter planes noticed so many Israeli troops gathering for the concert that they reported the Israelis were massing for a new attack—and the concert proved to be a diversionary tactic.

The concert was held outdoors amid some ancient ruins. At sunset, Bernstein played a moving rendition of a Mozart piano concerto and George Gershwin's *Rhapsody in Blue*, surrounded by 5000 weary but grateful troops.

At a concert in a hall in the city of Rehovot, two air-raid alarms sounded. Bernstein was conducting and playing a Beethoven piano concerto when the alarm went off. He kept right on playing and the audience didn't move.

Later, someone praised his performance under such trying circumstances. He replied jokingly, "I never played such an adagio. I thought it was my swan song."

Besides touring with the Israel Philharmonic, Leonard spent many evenings entertaining in hospitals and military bases. He seemed to thrive on the hectic and difficult schedule.

The grateful government of Israel awarded him the Emblem of the Defenders of Jerusalem for his courage and service to its people. Since then, he has returned many times to conduct the Israel Philharmonic, and has maintained close ties.

Bernstein toured the country of Israel with the Israel Philharmonic Orchestra, often performing dangerously close to the firing lines. The new nation was fighting for its life, and at one point Bernstein played a concert for the combat troops in the fighting zone (left).

Baldwin

"Ven my stick touches de air, you play."

Back in New York, things weren't going very well with the New York City Symphony. Principally because of Bernstein's improvements, attendance had increased considerably at the orchestra's concerts. He hoped for an increased budget to schedule more programs, increase salaries of the orchestra members, and make other improvements. Instead, the management announced it would cut the budget further. Bernstein promptly submitted his letter of resignation as director. The announcement created a furor in New York, but Bernstein refused to withdraw his resignation without a commitment from the city to increase the orchestra's budget. The money was not forthcoming, despite bargaining and promises, and eventually the New York City Symphony folded.

Bernstein kept busy conducting and composing. He completed his second symphony, the *Age of Anxiety,* a serious, complex work based on W. H. Auden's poem of the same name. He worked on the ambitious project while on concert tour, completing parts in Taos, Philadelphia, Richmond, and Tel Aviv. The finishing touches were applied during a month-long tour with the Pittsburgh Symphony and the last bar completed, as Bernstein noted on the score, "NYC—the first day of Spring!"

Bernstein described the work as a record of the difficult and problematical search for faith, the subject of Auden's poem. The music has great variety, ranging from jazz to twelve-tone technique to sweeping romanticism. Only a composer with the superb craftsmanship of Bernstein could have successfully united these disparate elements. Many critics called the symphony his most interesting score.

Dedicated to Serge Koussevitzky, the symphony received its world premiere in Boston on April 8, 1949, under Koussevitzky's baton with Bernstein as piano soloist. Leonard was awarded the $1000 Hornblit Prize when the *Age of Anxiety* was chosen as the best new work presented that year by the Boston Symphony. Two years later Jerome Robbins produced a ballet with the same title.

Fame had not spoiled Leonard, and he continued to work harder than ever at his music.

Back in New York, the New York City Symphony was on the verge of collapse. The management announced that the budget would again be cut, and Bernstein submitted a letter of resignation. He kept busy conducting and composing and completed his second symphony, the Age of Anxiety, *which he dedicated to Serge Koussevitzky (opposite). The symphony, conducted by Koussevitzky with Bernstein as piano soloist, received its world premiere in 1949.*

Tragedy and Triumph

The year 1951 brought important changes to Leonard Bernstein's life. Fame had placed many demands on his time, but he continued to work as hard as ever. He still found time to enjoy life with boyish enthusiasm—attending parties, getting together with friends, and indulging in his wide variety of interests. He remained close to his family and old friends and saw them whenever he could.

Tragedy entered his life in June, while he was on a vacation in Mexico and beginning work on a light opera to be called *Trouble in Tahiti*. He received word that his idol, friend, and benefactor, Serge Koussevitzky, was dying in a Boston hospital. Bernstein dropped all his plans and rushed back to Boston as soon as he received the message. He arrived in time to spend most of one night with the old maestro, and they had a long talk about past years. Koussevitzky had hoped that his young protege would succeed him as conductor of the distinguished Boston Symphony, but this was not to be. Charles Munch had been brought in from Paris to succeed him. Koussevitzky felt keenly disappointed in this, and he would not live

In 1951, tragedy entered Leonard Bernstein's life when he received word that his idol, friend, and benefactor, Serge Koussevitzky, was dying in a Boston hospital. Bernstein left his Mexican vacation and rushed back to Boston in time to spend most of one night with the old maestro.

to see Leonard's brilliant future. It was a sad parting, and the next day Koussevitzky died.

Lenny was grief-stricken, and he realized that his loss was one that was irreplaceable. He stated many times later that he owed more to Koussevitzky than to any other man on earth.

One of the things Koussevitzky had loved most of all was the school at Tanglewood. Now Leonard suddenly realized that the opening for the 1951 season was less than a month away. He knew that he could not return to sunny Mexico nor finish his opera at this time when Tanglewood's conducting department needed him to take over as director. He headed for Tanglewood immediately.

Bernstein delivered a moving tribute to Koussevitzky at the opening Tanglewood concert. Later in the season, he led the Boston Symphony Orchestra in a performance of the *Missa Solemnis* as a tribute to the great conductor's memory. It was a beautiful, inspired performance, and an unforgettable occasion for those who heard it.

While still in the depths of sadness and loneliness, Leonard's life now took another turn. He was driving from New York to Tanglewood in August of 1951 with a lovely girl named Felicia Montealegre Cohn, whom he had known for several years. In fact, they had been engaged at one time, but it had not lasted. Now they stopped for dinner at a small inn along the way and suddenly Lenny proposed to her. They announced their engagement the next day.

Felicia, a slender, petite, beautiful girl, was a resident of Santiago, Chile. Her father was an American business executive who headed a large branch plant in Chile. She had come to New York to become an actress and study piano with the famous Chilean pianist, Claudio Arrau. Through him she had met Lenny, and they had immediately been attracted to each other. Not many months later they had become engaged, but they were both pursuing careers and traveling, and it didn't seem to work out. They broke off the engagement and saw each other only infrequently during the next four years. But now the time had come in Lenny's life when he felt he no longer wanted to be alone. He began courting Felicia again a few months before his proposal, and they both felt certain that marriage was what they wanted.

They were married less than a month after Lenny's proposal, in his boyhood place of worship, Temple Mishkan Tefile, in Boston. They then left for Mexico, where Bernstein intended to take a year-long sabbatical to compose, rest, and ponder his future. He cleared his schedule of conducting dates. The idyllic Mexican existence was again cut short, however, when Charles Munch was taken ill and Lenny was asked to return to Boston to substitute for him for several performances with the Boston Symphony.

While still in the depths of sadness and loneliness at the death of his friend Koussevitzky, Leonard's life took another turn. He became engaged to Felicia Montealegre Cohn, whom he had known for several years. Leonard and Felicia (opposite) were married less than a month after their engagement was announced.

Almost exactly a year after their marriage, the Bernsteins became the proud parents of a daughter, Jamie. Earlier that summer, Leonard's completed opera, *Trouble in Tahiti,* was presented at Brandeis University near Boston, where he had been appointed director of the School of Creative Arts. Later the work was presented on television and produced on Broadway.

As a faculty member at Brandeis, Bernstein lectured and taught a course in composition at the graduate level. The Bernsteins made their home in New York and for two years he made weekly, then monthly, trips to the Boston area for the classes. Finally he had to give them up, because Leonard felt that with his long intervals of absence, his students received no continuity in their instruction. He was too busy with projects in New York to devote more time to teaching. His classes and lectures were brilliant and stimulating—a forerunner to the excellence he would show as a teacher on his famous television programs. It appeared that everything Lenny tried he did well, but he was trying too many things at once to keep up with all of them. His friends in the music world knew he could be counted on to fill in on short notice and to do a beautiful job substituting for anybody.

Five weeks before rehearsal time, for instance, Betty Comden, Adolph Green, and Leonard Bernstein were asked to write the lyrics and music for a musical adaptation of Ruth McKenney's comedy, *My Sister Eileen.* Bernstein's schedule was already jammed with conducting dates and other projects, but he became interested in the project and took it on. Fourteen songs were written with lyrics by Comden and Green, and Bernstein finished the score in time for the rehearsals.

The result was *Wonderful Town,* which opened on Broadway in February, 1953. Starring Rosalind Russell, it ran 533 performances and won the Drama Critics Award for the year's best musical. Bernstein's score for the show won him both the Antoinette Perry and Donaldson awards. Among the well-remembered songs from the show were: "A Quiet Girl," "The Wrong-Note Rag," and "Ohio."

Almost exactly a year after their marriage, the Bernsteins became the proud parents of a daughter, Jamie, shown at left with her parents.

In 1953, Leonard Bernstein became the first American-born conductor ever to perform during the regular season of the world-famous opera, La Scala, in Milan, Italy. He conducted Medea, *with the brilliant, temperamental Maria Callas (left) singing the title role.*

Fortunately, Lenny now had some help from an old friend in keeping straight the tangled arrangements for his hectic schedule. Back in 1944, when he had first become a celebrity, he had suddenly become the recipient of innumerable phone calls, tons of mail, and telegrams. With his worldwide travels and conducting dates, there were many arrangements to be made, and he was at a loss to know how to handle them. He turned, as he had years ago, to Helen Coates for advice and help. He asked her if she would consider leaving Boston to become his personal assistant and secretary in New York. His one-time piano teacher happily agreed. She had watched his meteoric rise in music with pride, but hardly astonishment. She had expected it from the time he had studied under her for six dollars a lesson. With her to handle the complex details surrounding his life, he now had a trusted and dear friend who would help free him to concentrate on his career.

Lenny continued to plunge into projects that would have frightened other conductors. In 1953 he became the first American-born conductor ever to perform during the regular season of the world-famous citadel of opera, La Scala, in Milan, Italy. He was on a concert tour in Europe when La Scala lost its conductor for the opening performance of the season. Its management followed Bernstein from Milan to Florence to Rome, asking him to conduct *Medea,* with the brilliant, temperamental Maria Callas singing the title role.

Bernstein was understandably hesitant. He had conducted no major opera and he didn't know the score of *Medea.* But he was fascinated with opera, and here was a chance to experience it at the very top level. Very few conductors would want to risk their reputations in such a venture, but Leonard agreed to do it.

To make matters worse, there were only five days remaining before the performance. And in Milan awaited an orchestra whose members spoke no English, a new score to learn, and a diva of Maria Callas' monumental temperament. To top things off, Leonard had bronchitis and an allergy and he alternated between coughing and sneezing.

Bernstein's linguistic ability solved the language problem; his brilliance at sight reading helped him to master the score, and he hit it off well with Callas from the start. He discovered that she was as energetic and as much of a perfectionist as he was, and each respected the other. The performance, judged even by La Scala's exacting standards, was a huge success. Leonard shared several curtain bows with Callas, and the audience stood and cheered. Now Lenny was more fascinated than ever with opera, and he hoped to find the time some day to work with it.

Next he completed another major concert work called *Serenade*. It was a five-movement work for violin, strings, and percussion and Leonard himself conducted its world premiere, with Isaac Stern as soloist, at the Venice Festival in Italy. Herbert Ross later produced a ballet from it, *Serenade for Seven*.

Leonard also experienced writing a movie score, something he had wanted to try. It was the music for the dramatic film *On the Waterfront*, starring Marlon Brando. The score was impressive enough to be nominated for an academy award, and Leonard felt satisfied that it heightened the drama in the film considerably.

This was the same year in which he made his historic first *Omnibus* telecast and whetted the appetites of millions of Americans who knew little about concert music or conductors named Leonard Bernstein. His subsequent Young People's programs, which have continued to this day, built up a tremendous audience.

On these shows, Bernstein discussed a wide range of music topics—from titans like Beethoven, Bach, and Mozart to subjects like rhythm, tonality, romanticism, jazz, opera, musical comedy, modern music, and conducting. And since he wrote his own material, the programs had that wonderful, fresh Bernstein flair—his rightness and choice of figures of speech that caught the essence of his ideas and made complex points clear. He used the notes of a composition, analogies, humor, visual aids of all kinds and, of course, music itself. But the most important ingredient was Leonard Bernstein himself—his articulate manner and the genuine love of music that he managed to convey to the television screen.

Fortunately, the scripts of many of these programs have been printed in Bernstein's absorbing books on music: *The Joy of Music, The Infinite Variety of Music,* and *Leonard Bernstein's Young People's Concerts for Reading and Listening*. Readers who saw the telecasts years ago are able to "take refresher courses" by reading the books, which also contain fascinating material that has been praised by critics. Bernstein's wit, informality, and enthusiasm show through in his writing, too.

Leonard and his wife Felicia were overjoyed on July 7, 1955, when a son

"...I wish I could convey to you the excitement and insane joy of it, which nothing else touches..."

was born to them. They named him Alexander Serge, honoring the memory of Koussevitzky. They now lived in a large New York apartment on West 57th Street that included a studio for Leonard. He called it his "thinking room" and had it painted gray with no windows to distract him. Sometimes he would play the piano there, but often he would simply lie on a couch, getting the germ of an idea for a composition.

Bernstein has often said that a creative idea can just happen, anywhere and at any time. It comes from within a person, not as a consciously conceived thing, he points out. He once described it to a University of Chicago audience:

"I wish I could convey to you the excitement and insane joy of it, which nothing else touches... nothing touches the extraordinary, jubilant sensation of being caught up in this thing—so that you're not just inside yourself, not just lying there. Let's say you get an idea and go to the piano and you start with it; and you don't know where you're going to go next, and then you're doing something else next, and you can't stop doing the next thing, and you don't know why. It's madness and it's marvelous. There's nothing in the world like it."

This statement might be applied to Leonard Bernstein's whole remarkable career. He has gone on from one achievement to another, so enthusiastically that he probably hasn't paused to determine why he took each step.

Two more important steps in that career lay ahead of him in the year 1957.

Tribute to a Genius

After the almost unbelievable series of successes that had been enjoyed by Leonard Bernstein during his career, it was only natural that somewhere along the line one of his projects would be a failure. This happened, relatively speaking, with a Broadway musical for which he wrote the score in 1956—*Candide*. Based on the Voltaire novel of the same name, it seemed to lack audience-drawing appeal. Some critics felt that the eighteenth-century philosophical tale was not well-suited to the theater. Bernstein's music was well received by the critics, however, and later the London presentation proved popular. The *Candide* album was a tremendous success.

But the failure of *Candide* was quickly followed by Bernstein's greatest Broadway success, *West Side Story*, which opened at the Winter Garden Theater on September 26, 1957. It was destined to rank with the greatest musicals in the history of Broadway theater.

The idea for *West Side Story* began with Leonard's collaborator, Jerome Robbins, suggesting a modern version of the story of Romeo and Juliet. Another friend, Arthur Laurents, who would eventually write the book, was discussing the juvenile gang warfare in New York with Bernstein one day. They began to talk about the problems of the Puerto Rican immigrants in a strange land, and their tensions and conflicts. Soon their ideas had crystallized into a story line with the Romeo and Juliet theme. The story would be set in New York's slums and would focus on the rivalries of two gangs: the Jets, a group of American-born kids, and the Sharks, a group of young Puerto Ricans. Tony, a co-founder of the Jets who is maturing and beginning to lose his taste for gang activities, meets and falls in love with Maria, the sister of Bernardo, the leader of the Sharks. Their love, like Romeo's and Juliet's, is destined for tragedy from the very beginning. The tenderness of

---

In September of 1957, Bernstein's greatest Broadway success, West Side Story, *opened at the Winter Garden Theater. It was destined to rank with the greatest musicals in the history of Broadway theater. The idea for the show began with Leonard's collaborator, Jerome Robbins, suggesting a modern version of the story of Romeo and Juliet. It gradually grew into a story set in New York's slums focusing on the rivalries of two gangs, one American-born boys and one Puerto Rican. Opposite, dancers rehearse before the show's opening.*

In this scene, members of West Side Story's *rival gangs, the Sharks and the Jets, rehearse a fight as the various directors look on. Collaboration on the show was long and painstaking. Arthur Laurents wrote the story, Bernstein the score, Jerome Robbins directed the show and was assisted in choreography by Peter Gennaro. The lyrics were written by Stephen Sondheim.*

CHINESE
WEST SIDE STORY
WEST SIDE STORY
PANAVISION 70
TECHNICOLOR

The photograph at left shows one of the many theater marquees across the nation that advertised West Side Story *during record runs. It had been made into a successful motion picture after 734 performances on Broadway.*

the love between Tony and Maria becomes all the more touching when it is set against the hatred, violence, and tension swirling around them. The story thus combines the appeal of a timeless classic story with a significant social commentary of American life.

Collaboration on the show was long and painstaking. In addition to Laurents writing the story and Bernstein the score, Jerome Robbins directed the show and was assisted in choreography by Peter Gennaro. The lyrics were written by Stephen Sondheim, a young composer and writer. No established stars were used, and the young actors and dancers doubled as vocalists as well.

The play was an outstanding success, excellent in every area. It was realistic, believable, and made a relevant social comment. The tough slum-gang language and the raw violence enacted by the talented young cast brought the show crackling to life.

Bernstein's brilliant music reflected the bitterness and frustrations of slum life, and it underscored the brief tenderness of the doomed lovers. Leonard had often fretted over the fact that he hadn't written a "hit tune." This was no longer true when the public heard the lovely songs from *West Side Story*. Some of them, such as "Maria," "Tonight," "Somewhere," and "I Feel Pretty" have already become popular classics.

The show ran on Broadway for 734 performances and was made into a successful motion picture. Critics have hailed it as a milestone in Broadway musicals—a play of beauty that also has substance and significance.

But as satisfying as this artistic and popular success was to Leonard Bernstein, he earned another distinction that year that was even more satisfying. His friend Dimitri Mitropoulos, who had been musical director of the New York Philharmonic for several years, decided to retire. After sharing the conducting duties for a year, Leonard was appointed musical director of the Philharmonic.

As satisfying as the success of West Side Story *had been to Leonard Bernstein, he earned another distinction that was even more satisfying. His friend Dimitri Mitropoulos decided to retire and Leonard was appointed musical director of the New York Philharmonic, after having shared for a year the conducting duties of that orchestra. Bernstein and Mitropoulos are shown at right at the time of the appointment.*

"We worshipped Toscanini but we love Lenny."

Thus he became the only man of American birth to hold this position and, at forty-one, one of the youngest conductors in the orchestra's history. He now joined the distinguished roster of Philharmonic maestros that included Gustav Mahler, Arturo Toscanini, Artur Rodzinski, and Bernstein's friend and benefactor, Mitropoulos, who twenty-one years ealier had encouraged Leonard to become a conductor.

Odd as it may seem, Leonard was not certain at first that he wanted the directorship. He wanted more time to compose and knew the Philharmonic would, at the very least, be a consuming, full-time job.

When he did accept the position, he didn't take the honor lightly. He announced that the Philharmonic would be his full-time job. This, of course, meant that he would have to cancel some of his other plans, which he did.

On October 1, 1958, Bernstein began the first of the many innovations that were to mark his tenure as musical director. On that day he began the Thursday evening "Preview Concerts." At these he would speak about the composers whose works the orchestra was performing, sing and play the piano between numbers, and often present works that had rarely been performed before. In these informal "dress rehearsals" he would joke about his singing and playing. The audiences loved it, and the concerts were sellouts. The same proved true of his Saturday morning Young Peoples' Concerts.

One of Leonard's major tasks was to win the loyalty and respect of the musicians, and he proved equal to it. They respected his musical knowledge and brilliance, and he soon won them over with his engaging personality. He cared little for formality, and many of the musicians call him "Lenny" to this day. As one of them put it, "we worshipped Toscanini, but we love Lenny."

Under Bernstein's leadership, the Philharmonic thrived. It seemed to be a different orchestra with a new sound, and critics praised it. Attendance soared and television performances were willingly sponsored.

Bernstein took the Philharmonic on a triumphal tour of South and Central America in 1958, and the response was so gratifying that an even longer tour was planned in 1959 for Europe, Russia, and the Middle East. This tour lasted ten weeks, in which the Philharmonic gave fifty concerts in seventeen countries. All Europe praised both the orchestra and its conductor, but it was in the Soviet Union that the enthusiasm was the greatest. The orchestral group succeeded in spreading incalcuable good will for America.

When the Philharmonic returned to the United States, a special ceremony was held in Washington for Bernstein

ЭКСКУРСИИ по ВЫСТАВКАМ МУЗЕЯ
ХРАНИЛИЩА МУЗЕЯ
открыты для посетителей
ГОСУДАРСТВЕННЫЙ
МУЗЕЙ
МУЗЫКАЛЬНОЙ КУЛЬТУРЫ

Under Bernstein's leadership, the Philharmonic thrived. It seemed to be a different orchestra with a new sound; critics praised it, attendance soared, television performances were sponsored, and the orchestra's financial picture brightened. In 1959, Bernstein took the orchestra on a tour of Europe, Russia, and the Middle East. All Europe praised the orchestra and its conductor, but it was in the Soviet Union that the enthusiasm was the greatest. The pictures on page 82 were taken in Moscow during Bernstein's appearances there. On his return, Bernstein discussed the triumphant tour at a meeting of the National Press Club (left).

and the orchestra. It was one of many honors that Leonard and his orchestra have earned in the past several years from all over the world.

Perhaps the most treasured individual honor for Bernstein came on February 13, 1961, when the Philharmonic itself honored its conductor at its Pension Fund Benefit. As he looked on from a box in Carnegie Hall, an all-Bernstein program was presented, with his old friends Adolph Green and Betty Comden serving as masters of ceremonies. Aaron Copland led the orchestra in the Overture to *Candide*. He was followed by Vladimir Golschmann conducting the *Jeremiah Symphony* performance with Jennie Tourel as soloist. Lukas Foss conducted a new suite of nine symphonic dances from *West Side Story*. The performance ended with scenes, staged and costumed, from *On the Town*, *Wonderful Town*, *Candide*, *Fancy Free*, and *West Side Story*. It was a deeply moving tribute.

Almost exactly a year after this, on February 28, 1962, a second daughter, Nina, was born to the Bernsteins.

Bernstein has kept his word about making the New York Philharmonic his full-time job, and he has worked hard to achieve the great progress he has made with the orchestra. But this routine will be altered in the near future. He will resign as musical director at the completion of the 1968-1969 season. It will mark his tenth year as conductor. At a still-youthful age he will continue to be associated with the orchestra, conducting several weeks during the regular season in the position of Laureate Conductor, a lifetime post and title created especially for him in honor of his great services. And he will continue to arrange and conduct the orchestra's Young People's Concerts.

Perhaps one of the greatest honors for Bernstein came when the Philharmonic itself honored its conductor in February, 1961. As he looked on from a box in Carnegie Hall, an all-Bernstein program was presented, with his friends Adolph Green and Betty Comden serving as masters of ceremonies. Aaron Copland (opposite) conducted the overture to Candide, *and many other performers contributed to the program.*

But he will be free of the tremendous responsibility of being musical director, and he can go back to composing and any other activities he likes.

Bernstein has said he regrets that a decade has gone by without his being able to take up composing where he left off with *West Side Story.* He feels strongly that he can contribute to evolving a new kind of theater form, and that *West Side Story* was a step in that direction.

Not many figures in the music world would step down from a pinnacle such as the conductor's job with the New York Philharmonic. But Leonard Bernstein has never been typical. He is a restless, brilliant musician who wants to conquer more than one world. He has established his reputation as a great conductor, but there are other frontiers to cross. He has made his mark as a pianist and a composer, but there are other ideas for him to express. Leonard Bernstein's quest is perfection as an artist, and his destiny appears to be near that goal.

Leonard Bernstein has worked hard to achieve the great progress he has made with the New York Philharmonic. This routine will be altered, however, for Bernstein will resign as musical director at the completion of the 1968-1969 season. He will continue to conduct several weeks during the season and will continue to arrange and conduct the orchestra's Young People's Concerts. But he will also have time to compose and possibly make more recordings than he has been able to in the past. Right: Bernstein listens to a playback after a recording session.

Summary

The geniuses and near-geniuses who play the leading roles in the world of serious music seldom can communicate with the average citizen. Their total absorption in their art usually narrows their personalities and the non-musical person finds it difficult to identify with them. The rich beauty of classical music has been denied many people who have thought it the remote world of the privileged and specially educated.

It was the destiny of a young American musician of incredible talent to tear down the barriers and bring the simple joy of music to millions. Leonard Bernstein did this with a freshness, an enthusiasm, and a naturalness that had never before been seen in such a highly placed figure in the music world. He was the man of the hour, a twentieth-century American musician who used a twentieth-century medium—television—to reach the public. His appeal to young people could not be duplicated by older, more formal personalities. If America was ready at this point in history for a great widening of cultural knowledge, Leonard Bernstein was equally ready to fulfill his destiny as the man best qualified to accomplish it. His preparation for this role had been long and difficult, marked by hard work, defeats, and disappointments. His great natural talent had been tempered by discipline and training, and he emerged as America's most highly qualified musician—a pianist, conductor, and composer whose stature would show the world that his country had taken its place in the history of great music.

Opposite: Bernstein and his wife Felicia in 1959.

Overleaf: Bernstein and his secretary and former music teacher, Helen Coates, at Lincoln Center, New York City, in May, 1967.

Bibliography

BARRETT, M. "Five Careers of Leonard Bernstein." *Reader's Digest*, May, 1960.

"Baton For Bernstein." *Time*, January 13, 1958.

BAUER, MARION. *Twentieth Century Music*. New York: G. P. Putnam's, 1947.

BRIGGS, JOHN. *Leonard Bernstein, The Man, His Work, and His World*. New York: World, 1961.

BERNSTEIN, B. "Leonard Bernstein's Separate Peace With Berlin." *Esquire*, October, 1961.

BERNSTEIN, LEONARD. *The Joy of Music*. New York: Simon & Schuster, 1959.

———. *The Infinite Variety of Music*. New York: Simon & Schuster, 1966.

———. "What Makes Music American?" *McCalls*, October, 1962.

———. "What Makes Opera Grand." *Vogue*, December, 1958.

———. "Speaking of Music." *Atlantic*, December, 1957.

———. "What I Mean By Musical Meaning." *New Republic*, June 9, 1958.

"Boy With Cheek." *Time*, February 7, 1964.

"Busy Time For a Young Maestro." *Life*, January 7, 1957.

EWEN, DAVID. *Leonard Bernstein*. Philadelphia: Chelton, 1960.

———. *The Complete Book of Twentieth Century Music*. New Jersey: Prentice-Hall, 1965 ed.

"Giant and a Prince." *Time*, February 8, 1963.

HAGGIN, B. H. "Composer and Conductor." *New Republic*, August 8, 1964.

HARRIS, ELEANOR. "The Happy Genius." *Saturday Evening Post*, June 16, 1956.

HARRISON, J. "Making A Record With L. Bernstein." *Reporter*, July 11, 1957.

HUGHES, A. "Leonard Bernstein." *Musical American*, January, 1961.

KLEIN, HOWARD. "Recordings: A New Door Has Opened for Leonard Bernstein." *New York Times*, November 20, 1960.

KOLODIN, I. "At Home With Leonard Bernstein." *Saturday Review*, October 18, 1958.

———. "One For The Road." *Saturday Review*, April 25, 1964.

KOLODIN, I. "Summer Nights at the Philharmonic." *Saturday Review*, July 31, 1965.

LAURENCE, R. "Professor Bernstein's Required Readings." *Hi Fi*, December, 1965.

LINDSAY, DAVID. "The Remarkable Mr. Bernstein." *Coronet*, December, 1956.

MEHLING, H., and A. ROBIN. "Living Legends." *Today's Health*, September, 1959.

MOOR, PAUL. "Leonard Bernstein: Ceiling Unlimited." *Harper's*, February, 1948.

MORTON, EREDINE. "Exceptional Musician." *Holiday*, October, 1959.

"Mr. Bernstein of Lincoln Center." *Newsweek*, September 24, 1962.

"One, Get L. B." *Newsweek*, March 17, 1962.

"Portrait." *Musical American*, December 1, 1957.

For a complete list of recordings by and of Leonard Bernstein, see *Briggs*, 259-267.

RICE, ROBERT. "The Pervasive Musician." *New Yorker*, January 11, 1958 and January 18, 1958, two parts.

RICHMOND, JOHN. "Portrait of a Genius." *Tomorrow*, May, 1945.

RODDY, JOSEPH. "Who Lives at Carnegie Hall?" *Hi Fi*, February, 1959.

SCHOENBERG, HAROLD. "New Job For The Protean Mr. Bernstein." New York *Times Magazine*, December 17, 1957.

SCHOENBERG, HAROLD. "What Bernstein Is Doing To The Philharmonic." *Harper's*, May, 1959.

———. "Bernstein: Wrong Time to Leave?" New York *Times*, November 15, 1966.

"So The Young May Feel." *Newsweek*, March 2, 1959.

SCHUBART, MARK. "A Triple Note Man of the Music World." New York *Times Magazine*, January 28, 1945.

STEINBERG, WILLIAM. "Conducting: A Misunderstood Art." New York *Herald Tribune*, December 27, 1964.

"Wunderkind." *Time*, February 4, 1957.

Index